Chroma
TAROT

Uncover the symbolism and significance of every card.
Explore straightforward spreads for decision-making, relationships, insight, and divergence.
Immerse yourself in mastering the entire deck through an enjoyable and engaging approach.
This journey will not only enhance your understanding of Tarot but also make the learning
process a fulfilling experience.

COLORING BOOK

BY

J.C MENDRYGA

CONTENTS

DEDICATION

FOR
ADELIA MENDRYGA

THIS BOOK BELONGS TO:

FORDWARD

In my initial encounter with the Rider Waite Tarot almost five decades ago, the vibrant illustrations on the cards immediately captured my attention. The idea of embarking on a journey of self-discovery and gaining insights into others through the manipulation of cardboard pieces fascinated me deeply. What drew me in was the Tarot's pure and open essence, reminiscent of the Fool card.

Engaging in the act of coloring, much like the empowering will of the Magician, became a transformative experience to channel energies. Despite facing initial challenges and almost succumbing to the daunting task of memorizing card meanings, I found salvation in courses on theatrical improvisation and literary symbolism. These courses provided me with the necessary tools to weave metaphorically rich tales inspired by the Tarot images.

Yearning for a hands-on, multisensory approach to learning, I authored books that shared the methods which had aided my own understanding. However, I acknowledged that text-heavy resources posed challenges for some, hindering a deeper connection.

This book exceeds my initial expectations; simply labeling it as a coloring book would be an understatement. It offers a holistic immersion into the Tarot, where the accompanying text for each card subtly sparks the imagination and evokes personal associations, bringing the images to life beneath your fingertips.

Consider yourself fortunate to have J.C. Mendryga as your guide on this Tarot exploration. He seamlessly blends a contemporary, practical approach with a compassionate heart, drawing from extensive experience in assisting numerous individuals with life's challenges. J.C. Mendryga focuses on real issues, generously sharing his wisdom for the benefit of the reader. Follow his example spreads, laying out cards from your own deck to fully grasp the essence of the Tarot.

Mendryga's concise and spirited advice, covering aspects from familiarizing yourself with the cards to navigating professional challenges, elevates this book to an indispensable, comprehensive resource for anyone delving into the profound realm of Tarot.

HOW TO USE THIS COLORING BOOK

This coloring book offers versatile ways to engage with its content. While my suggestions provide one approach, feel free to explore various methods that resonate with you. Your unique interpretation and creativity are key – embrace the freedom to make this coloring experience truly yours

Step 1: after you carefully colored your deck delicately cut it out, and remove it. remember to take your tim, and ensuring your deck aligns with your energy you want to infuse into your coloring Journey.

Step 2: Gather Your Coloring Supplies Assemble your coloring toolkit. Opt for colored pencils or crayons fo their versatility and control. Ensure you have a sharpener available for fine details. Lay out your chosen Tarot deck beside your coloring materials, creating a harmonious setup for your creative process

Step 3: Choose a Peaceful Time Select a time when you can immerse yourself in the coloring experience without distractions.

Dim the lights or bask in natural light for a soothing ambiance. Consider incorporating elements like scented candles or calming background music to enhance the serene atmosphere during your coloring session

Step 4: Set the Scene
Create a dedicated space for your coloring journey. Clear away any clutter and minimize external distractions. Arrange your Tarot deck, coloring supplies, and perhaps a journal or notebook for reflections. Tailor the setting to evoke a tranquil environment,

allowing you to fully engage in the creative process.

Step 5: Begin Coloring - Your Way
Approach the coloring process with an open mind. Choose a Tarot card that resonates with your current emotions or intentions.Start with light strokes, gradually building layers to capture the intricate details. Don't be bound by traditional color associations; let your intuition guide your choices. Embrace the freedom to interpret and color each card in a way that feels authentic to you. Remember, there's no right or wrong – it's your unique expression that matters most.

TAKE SOME TIME TO LOOK AT THE FINAL IMAGE.

What did you discover about the card?
What do you think is the core of it?
It's good to know the general meaning of each card. But when you are doing a Tarot reading, try to ignore what "the experts" say and trust your own intuition.
Take it easy and notice any thoughts that come up as you color along. Do some cards evoke strong feelings for you? Do some cards make you think of someone you know or a situation that's happening in your life right now?

Is the card sending you a specific message at this moment? Is there a lesson or story that you suddenly remember?
Look at the illustration for a while and then write down any thoughts, interpretations, or emotions that arise in the space after the description of each card or in a journal.
Appreciate your work, and then move on as you feel inspired.

A QUICK INTRO GOT QUESTIONS TAROT'S GOT THE ANSWER

What energies should I embrace in my life right now?
How can I overcome challenges on my current path?
What insights can Tarot provide about my relationships?
What opportunities or obstacles lie ahead in my career?
How can I enhance my spiritual growth and self-discovery?

Welcome to the mystical world of Tarot, where questions find answers in the language of symbols. Whether you're seeking guidance, introspection, or a touch of magic, Tarot's got you covered. Explore the cards, unravel the mysteries, and let the journey begin. Got questions? Tarot's got the answers.

Many hold the belief that within each person resides an innate capacity for intuition—a profound sense of knowing. These intuitive abilities often manifest as sudden flashes of insight or a distinctive feeling that arises unexpectedly. Embracing these moments involves acknowledging the unspoken wisdom within. Trusting these intuitive nudges can lead to profound insights, fostering a richer connection with one's inner self and providing a unique channel for understanding the complexities of life.

LET'S DELVE INTO THE PROFOUND SIGNIFICANCE OF COLORS IN THE WORLD OF TAROT

In the intricate realm of Tarot, colors transcend mere aesthetics; they become a language of symbols, conveying profound meanings and unlocking the gateways to deeper insights. Each color chosen for a Tarot card is a deliberate brushstroke on the canvas of divination, carrying its unique vibrational frequency and tapping into the subconscious.

Black: The enigmatic void, black signifies the mysteries concealed in the shadows. It beckons the seeker to explore the depths of the unknown, embracing transformation and the unseen aspects of life.

Blue: As the color of the vast sky and tranquil waters, blue resonates with spirituality and intuition. It beckons the seeker to dive into the realms of the mind, unlocking profound insights and connecting with higher truths.

Brown: Rooted in the earth's hues, brown grounds the Tarot imagery in practicality. It signifies stability, reliability, and the tangible foundations upon which life unfolds.

Gray: A delicate dance between black and white, gray embodies neutrality and balance. It serves as a bridge between opposites, encouraging the seeker to find harmony amidst conflicting forces.

Green: Nurtured by nature, green symbolizes growth and the heart's emotional landscape. It invites the seeker to explore the flourishing realms of feelings, fostering emotional equilibrium.

Orange: Radiating warmth and vitality, orange sparks enthusiasm and creativity. It ignites the fires of inspiration, encouraging the seeker to approach life with zest and positive energy.

Purple: Drenched in mysticism, purple links the seeker to spiritual awareness and higher consciousness. It unveils the unseen realms, inviting exploration into the divine mysteries.

Red: A fervent flame, red embodies passion and life force energy. It propels the seeker into action, infusing vigor and dynamism into their journey.

Silver: Illuminated by the moon's glow, silver taps into intuitive energies. It reflects emotional stability, connecting the seeker with the subtle whispers of the subconscious.

White: Pure and luminous, white epitomizes clarity and spiritual enlightenment. It serves as a beacon, guiding the seeker towards higher realms of understanding.

Yellow: Radiating the brilliance of the sun, yellow illuminates the intellectual domain. It symbolizes joy, optimism, and the active, enlightened mind.

HERE ARE TEN WAYS YOU CAN INTEGRATE TAROT INTO YOUR EVERYDAY LIFE:

1. Self-Reflection: Use tarot cards for daily introspection, gaining insights into your emotions, thoughts, and actions.

2. Decision-Making: Consult the cards when facing choices or decisions to gain additional perspectives and guidance.

3. Goal Setting: Incorporate tarot into your goal-setting process, gaining clarity on steps to take and potential obstacles.

4. Mindfulness Practice: Integrate tarot into mindfulness routines, fostering a deeper connection with the present moment.

5. Creative Inspiration: Draw a card for creative inspiration or overcoming creative blocks, sparking new ideas and perspectives

6. Journaling: Combine tarot with journaling, recording card pulls and reflections to track personal growth and patterns.

7. Meditation Focus: Use tarot cards as focal points for meditation sessions, allowing the imagery to deepen your contemplative experience.

8. Daily Guidance: Pull a card each morning for a daily dose of guidance, setting a positive and mindful tone for the day.

9. Conflict Resolution: When faced with conflicts, use tarot to gain insights into underlying issues and find constructive resolutions.

10. Gratitude Practice: End your day by drawing a card and reflecting on moments of gratitude, fostering a positive mindset.

MAJOR ARCADIA

The Arcadia tarot deck is a unique and beautiful collection of cards that draws inspiration from nature, mythology and art. The deck follows the traditional structure of the tarot with 78 cards, divided into Major and Minor Arcana. The Major Arcana cards represent the major themes and lessons of life, while the Minor Arcana cards reflect the everyday situations and challenges. Here are some of the Major Arcana cards and brief summaries:

THE FOOL

- Upright: New beginnings, spontaneity, innocence.
- Reversed: Foolishness, recklessness, missed opportunities.
- Zodiac: Uranus
- Animals: Dog
- Numerology: 0

THE MAGICIAN

- Upright: Manifestation, power, resourcefulness.
- Reversed: Manipulation, lack of direction, untapped talents.
- Zodiac: Mercury
- Animals: Falcon
- Numerology: 1

THE HIGH PRIESTESS

- Upright: Intuition, mystery, subconscious knowledge.
- Reversed: Hidden agendas, lack of intuition, secrets revealed.
- Zodiac: Moon
- Animals: Striped Owl
- Numerology: 2

THE EMPRESS

- Upright: Fertility, nurturing, abundance.
- Reversed: Neglect, dependence, stagnation.
- Zodiac: Venus
- Animals: Dolphin
- Numerology: 3

THE HIEROPHANT

- Upright: Tradition, spiritual guidance, conformity.
- Reversed: Rebellion, non-conformity, unconventional beliefs.
- Animals: Bull
- Astrology: Taurus
- Numerology: 5

THE EMPEROR

- Upright: Authority, structure, leadership.
- Reversed: Domineering, lack of control, chaos.
- Zodiac: Aries
- Animals: Ram
- Numerology: 4

THE CHARIOT

- Upright: Victory, determination, willpower.
- Reversed: Defeat, lack of direction, aggression.
- Zodiac: Cancer
- Animals: Sphinx
- Numerology: 7

THE LOVERS

- Upright: Love, union, choices.
- Reversed: Disharmony, imbalance, difficult decisions.
- Zodiac: Gemini
- Animals: Dove
- Numerology: 6

THE HERMIT

- Upright: Soul-searching, guidance, solitude.
- Reversed: Isolation, loneliness, withdrawal.
- Zodiac: Virgo
- Animals: Tortoise
- Numerology: 9

STRENGTH

- Upright: Inner strength, courage, compassion.
- Reversed: Weakness, self-doubt, lack of courage.
- Zodiac: Leo
- Animals: Lion
- Numerology: 8

WHEEL OF FORTUNE

- Upright: Destiny, cycles, change.
- Reversed: Bad luck, resistance to change, unexpected events.
- Zodiac: Jupiter
- Animals: Sphinx
- Numerology: 10

THE HANGED MAN

- Wheel of Fortune
- Upright: Destiny, cycles, change. Reversed: Bad luck, resistance to change, unexpected events. Zodiac: Jupiter Animals: Sphinx Numerology: 10

TEMPERANCE

- Upright: Balance, moderation, harmony.
- Reversed: Imbalance, excess, lack of moderation.
- Zodiac: Sagittarius
- Astrology: Fire
- Numerology: 14

THE TOWER

- Upright: Sudden change, upheaval, revelation. Reversed: Personal transformation, avoiding disaster, fear of change.
- Zodiac: Mars
- Astrology: Mars
- Numerology: 16

THE MOON

- Upright: Intuition, illusion, subconscious.
- Reversed: Confusion, fear, emotional upheaval.
- Zodiac: Pisces
- Astrology: Pisces
- Numerology: 18

JUDGMENT

- Upright: Rebirth, inner calling, forgiveness.
- Reversed: Self-doubt, refusal of self-examination, ignoring the call.
- Zodiac: Pluto
- Astrology: Pluto
- Numerology: 20

JUSTICE

- Upright: Fairness, truth, legal matters.
- Reversed: Unfairness, dishonesty, legal issues.
- Zodiac: Libra
- Astrology: Libra
- Numerology: 11

DEATH

- Upright: Transformation, new beginnings, endings.
- Reversed: Resistance to change, fear of the unknown, stagnation.
- Zodiac: Scorpio
- Astrology: Pluto
- Numerology: 13

THE DEVIL

- Upright: Temptation, bondage, materialism.
- Reversed: Release, enlightenment, overcoming addictions.
- Zodiac: Capricorn
- Astrology: Capricorn
- Numerology: 15

THE STAR

- Upright: Hope, inspiration, spiritual insight.
- Reversed: Lack of faith, despair, disappointment.
- Zodiac: Aquarius
- Astrology: Aquarius
- Numerology: 17

THE SUN

- Upright: Success, joy, vitality.
- Reversed: Negativity, inner child issues, feeling overshadowed.
- Zodiac: Sun
- Astrology: Sun
- Numerology: 19

THE WORLD

- Upright: Completion, fulfillment, unity.
- Reversed: Lack of completion, stagnation, unfulfilled potential.
- Zodiac: Saturn
- Astrology: Saturn
- Numerology: 21

0

THE FOOL

THE MAGICIAN

II

THE HIGH PRIESTESS

III

THE EMPRESS

IV

THE EMPEROR

V

THE HIEROPHANT

VI

THE LOVERS

VII

THE CHARIOT

VIII

STRENGTH

IX

THE HERMIT

X

WHEEL of FORTUNE

XI

JUSTICE

XII

THE HANGED MAN

XIII

DEATH

XIV

TEMPERANCE

XV

THE DEVIL

XVI

THE TOWER

XVII

THE STAR

XVIII

THE MOON

XIX

THE SUN

JUDGMENT

XXI

WORLD

THE WORLD

The Meaning of the Fool Arcana Tarot Card in Readings

The Fool is the first card of the Major Arcana in the tarot deck. It represents the beginning of a journey, a leap of faith, or a new adventure. The Fool is not bound by conventions, expectations, or fears. He is free to explore the unknown and discover new possibilities. The Fool is often associated with innocence, spontaneity, curiosity, and optimism. He does not worry about the consequences of his actions, but trusts in his intuition and the guidance of the universe.

The Fool can also indicate a lack of experience, maturity, or wisdom. He may be naive, reckless, or foolish. He may act impulsively, without considering the risks or the outcomes. He may be unaware of the dangers or challenges that lie ahead. He may be following a false or misleading path, or ignoring the advice of others. The Fool can also signify a need to break free from old patterns, habits, or beliefs that are holding him back. He may be ready to embrace a new perspective, a new identity, or a new way of life.

The Meaning of the Magician Arcana Tarot Card in Readings

The Magician Arcana Tarot Card is one of the most powerful and versatile cards in the deck. It represents the ability to manifest your desires, to use your skills and talents, and to create your own reality. The Magician is a master of the four elements: fire, water, air, and earth. He has access to all the tools he needs to achieve his goals: the wand, the cup, the sword, and the pentacle. He is confident, charismatic, and creative. He knows how to use his willpower, his intuition, his logic, and his resources.

The Magician Arcana Tarot Card can have different meanings depending on the context of the reading. In general, it signifies a time of action, initiative, and potential. It can indicate that you have the power to make things happen, that you are ready to start a new project or venture, or that you have a clear vision of what you want to accomplish. It can also suggest that you are learning new skills, developing your abilities, or discovering new aspects of yourself. The Magician encourages you to be proactive, optimistic, and resourceful.

However, the Magician Arcana Tarot Card also has a shadow side. It can warn you of being manipulative, deceptive, or arrogant. It can imply that you are using your power for selfish or unethical purposes, that you are overestimating your abilities, or that you are not being honest with yourself or others. It can also caution you of being distracted, scattered, or unfocused. The Magician reminds you to be mindful of your intentions, your actions, and your consequences.

The Meaning of The High Priestess Arcana Tarot Card in Readings

The High Priestess is the second card of the Major Arcana and represents the divine feminine, intuition, mystery and spirituality. She sits between two pillars, one black and one white, symbolizing the balance between opposites and the duality of nature. She holds a scroll with the word TORA, meaning the Greater Law, which is partly hidden, indicating that some secrets are only revealed to those who are ready. She wears a crown with a solar cross and a horned diadem, showing her connection to the earth and the heavens. She also wears a blue robe with a cross on her chest, signifying her sacred knowledge and authority. At her feet is a crescent moon, reflecting her link to the subconscious mind and the cycles of life.

The High Priestess appears in your readings when you need to tap into your inner wisdom and listen to your intuition rather than your rational mind. She invites you to explore the hidden realms of your soul and to access the spiritual enlightenment that awaits you there. She also reminds you that there is more to reality than what meets the eye, and that you can perceive the truth beyond the veil of illusion. The High Priestess is a card of mystery, silence and inner knowing. She asks you to trust your instincts and to follow your dreams.

The Meaning of The Empress Arcana Tarot Card in Readings

The Empress Arcana Tarot Card in Readings represents the feminine principle of creation, nurturing, abundance and beauty. She is often associated with the planet Venus, the goddess of love, and the element of earth, the source of life. The Empress is a mother figure who cares for her children and all living beings with compassion and generosity. She also symbolizes creativity, sensuality and fertility, as she expresses herself through various forms of art and pleasure. The Empress is a positive card that indicates growth, prosperity and harmony in one's life. She encourages you to connect with your inner nature and to appreciate the beauty and bounty of the world around you. Some more details about The Empress are:

- She wears a crown of twelve stars, showing her connection with the mystical realm and the cycles of the natural world.
- Her robe is patterned with pomegranates, symbolic of fertility, and sits upon a luxurious array of cushions and flowing red velvet.
- She is surrounded by a lush forest and a winding stream, signifying her connection with Mother Earth and life itself.
- In the foreground, golden wheat springs from the soil, reflecting abundance from a recent harvest.
- She is the source of all the Sun's energy, using strong solar energy to radiate life and blessings all around her.

The Meaning of The Emperor Arcana Tarot Card in Readings

The Emperor Arcana Tarot Card in Readings represents authority, leadership, and structure. It is the fourth card of the Major Arcana and symbolizes the masculine principle of order, discipline, and rationality. The Emperor is often depicted as a stern ruler on a throne, holding a scepter and an orb, with rams' heads as symbols of his connection to Aries and Mars. He is a powerful leader who commands respect and loyalty from his subjects. He creates law and order by applying principles and guidelines to any situation. He is also a father figure who provides protection, stability, and guidance to his loved ones.

The Emperor Arcana Tarot Card in Readings can indicate that you are adopting a leadership role in some aspect of your life, or that you are dealing with an authority figure who influences you. It can also suggest that you need to use your logic, focus, and discipline to achieve your goals and overcome any challenges. The Emperor Arcana Tarot Card in Readings can also represent a traditional relationship, where one partner takes on the role of the provider and protector, while the other partner follows their lead. However, this card also warns against being too rigid, domineering, or inflexible, as this can lead to conflict or resentment.

The Meaning of The Hierophant Arcana Tarot Card in Readings

The Hierophant is a card that represents the established spiritual values and beliefs of a group or an institution. It is often associated with religion, tradition, conformity and education. The Hierophant is the teacher or the guide who helps you access the divine wisdom and knowledge by following the rules and rituals of a certain system. He is the masculine counterpart of the High Priestess, who represents the intuitive and mystical aspects of spirituality.

When you see the Hierophant in a reading, it suggests that you have a desire or a need to follow a well-established process or an orthodox approach to your situation. You may benefit from working with a mentor, a teacher or a spiritual leader who can show you the way. You may also be involved in formal studies, ceremonies or rites of passage that are part of your spiritual journey. The Hierophant card encourages you to respect and honor the traditions and values of your community or culture.

However, the Hierophant can also indicate that you are too rigid or conformist in your beliefs and actions. You may be limiting yourself by adhering to the status quo or the expectations of others. You may need to challenge the existing structures or institutions that are holding you back from expressing your true self or exploring new paths. The Hierophant card invites you to question what you believe in and why, and to seek your own truth and freedom.

The Meaning of the Lovers Arcana Tarot Card in Readings

The Lovers is the sixth card of the Major Arcana in the tarot deck. It represents love, harmony, choice, and duality. The card shows a man and a woman standing before an angel, who blesses their union. The man looks at the woman, who looks at the angel, indicating a triangle of relationships. Behind the man is a tree of fire, symbolizing passion and desire. Behind the woman is a tree of fruit, symbolizing abundance and nourishment. Above them is a bright sun, signifying happiness and enlightenment.

The Lovers card can have different meanings depending on the context and the question. In general, it suggests that you are facing a decision that involves your heart and your values. You may have to choose between two lovers, two paths, or two aspects of yourself. The card advises you to listen to your intuition and follow your true feelings. The card also indicates that you are in a harmonious and loving relationship, or that you are about to meet someone who will change your life. The card encourages you to embrace love and trust in the divine guidance of the angel.

The Meaning of The Chariot Arcana Tarot Card in Readings

The Chariot is the seventh card of the Major Arcana in the tarot deck. It represents the power of will, determination, and self-control. The Chariot shows a person who is able to overcome obstacles and challenges by using their inner strength and confidence. The Chariot also symbolizes movement, progress, and success. The person who draws this card is likely to have a clear goal in mind and a strong drive to achieve it. They are not easily swayed by external influences or distractions. They are focused, disciplined, and motivated.

The Chariot can also indicate a journey, either physical or spiritual. The person may be traveling to a new destination, exploring new horizons, or embarking on a personal quest. The Chariot suggests that the person is in charge of their own destiny and has the ability to steer their life in the direction they want. The Chariot can also imply that the person needs to balance their rational and emotional sides, as well as their masculine and feminine energies. The Chariot is a card of action, initiative, and courage.

The Meaning of The Strength Arcana Tarot Card in Readings

The Strength card is a sign of inner power, confidence, and compassion. It suggests that you have the courage to face your fears and overcome any obstacles in your way. You are not easily swayed by external influences or pressures, but stay true to your own values and beliefs. You are also able to show kindness and empathy to others, even if they are different from you or oppose you. You have a balanced and harmonious relationship with yourself and others.

The Strength card advises you to tap into your inner resources and use them wisely. You have the potential to achieve great things, but you need to be mindful of how you express your energy and emotions. Do not let them overwhelm you or cause you to act impulsively or aggressively. Instead, channel them into constructive actions that benefit yourself and others. Be confident in your abilities, but also humble and grateful for what you have. Be compassionate towards yourself and others, but also assertive and firm when needed. By doing so, you will demonstrate your true strength and character.

The Meaning of The Hermit Arcana Tarot Card in Readings

The Hermit is a card of introspection, solitude and wisdom. It represents a time when you need to withdraw from the world and focus on your inner self. The Hermit can also indicate a spiritual quest, a search for truth and enlightenment. The Hermit can help you find your own path and guidance, but you have to be willing to listen to your intuition and follow your own light.

The Hermit can appear in readings when you are feeling lonely, isolated or misunderstood. It can also show up when you are facing a difficult decision or a challenge that requires careful thought and analysis. The Hermit advises you to take some time to reflect on your situation and your goals, and to seek the advice of a trusted mentor or teacher. The Hermit can also suggest that you need to be more self-reliant and independent, and not depend on others for validation or approval.

The Hermit is not a card of action, but of contemplation. It asks you to slow down and be patient, and to trust that the answers will come to you in due time. The Hermit can also warn you of the dangers of being too isolated or detached from reality. You need to balance your inner work with your outer interactions, and not lose touch with the people and the world around you. The Hermit can also encourage you to share your wisdom and insights with others, and to be a source of inspiration and guidance for those who seek your help.

The Meaning of Wheel of Fortune Arcana Tarot Card in Readings

The Wheel of Fortune is one of the most mysterious and powerful cards in the tarot deck. It represents the cycles of life, fate, karma, and destiny. The Wheel of Fortune reminds us that nothing is permanent, and that everything changes. Sometimes we are on top of the wheel, enjoying success and happiness, and sometimes we are at the bottom, facing challenges and difficulties. The Wheel of Fortune teaches us to accept the ups and downs of life with grace and wisdom, and to trust that the universe has a plan for us.

The Wheel of Fortune can also indicaate a turning point or a major change in your life. This can be positive or negative, depending on your situation and your attitude. The Wheel of Fortune encourages you to be flexible and adaptable, and to embrace the opportunities that come your way. The Wheel of Fortune can also signify luck, fortune, or synchronicity. You may experience a stroke of luck or a coincidence that leads you to your desired outcome. The Wheel of Fortune asks you to be open to the unexpected and to follow your intuition.

The Wheel of Fortune is a card of destiny and free will. You have the power to shape your own fate, but you are also subject to the laws of the universe. The Wheel of Fortune reminds you that what goes around comes around, and that you reap what you sow. The Wheel of Fortune advises you to act with integrity and responsibility, and to align yourself with your higher purpose. The Wheel of Fortune is a card of learning and growth. You can use the lessons from the past to create a better future for yourself and others.

The Meaning of Justice Arcana Tarot Card in Readings

The Justice card represents the concept of balance, fairness, and karma. It indicates that you are facing a situation where you need to make a decision based on logic, facts, and evidence. It also suggests that you are accountable for your actions and that you will experience the consequences of your choices, whether good or bad.

The Justice card can have different meanings depending on the context of the reading and the position of the card. For example, if the card appears in the past position, it may indicate that you have faced a legal issue, a contract, or a settlement in the past. If the card appears in the present position, it may indicate that you are dealing with a situation that requires honesty, integrity, and impartiality. If the card appears in the future position, it may indicate that you will receive justice, compensation, or recognition for your efforts.

The Justice card can also have different meanings depending on the question you ask and the aspect of your life you are focusing on. For example, if you ask about your career, the card may indicate that you need to be fair and ethical in your work environment, or that you will be rewarded or evaluated for your performance. If you ask about your love life, the card may indicate that you need to balance your needs and desires with those of your partner, or that you will face a decision that will affect your relationship. If you ask about your health, the card may indicate that you need to take care of your physical and mental well-being, or that you will undergo a medical procedure or a diagnosis.

The Justice card is a powerful and positive card that encourages you to act with integrity, responsibility, and wisdom. It reminds you that you have the power to create your own destiny and that you will reap what you sow.

The Meaning of The Hanged Man Arcana Tarot Card in Readings

This card is often misunderstood or feared, but it actually has a positive message for those who are willing to see things from a different perspective.

The Hanged Man represents a state of surrender, sacrifice, and enlightenment. It suggests that you may need to let go of your old beliefs, habits, or attachments, and embrace a new way of thinking or being. The Hanged Man invites you to pause, reflect, and meditate on your situation, and to trust that the universe has a higher plan for you.

The Hanged Man can also indicate a time of transition, transformation, or initiation. You may be undergoing a spiritual awakening, or experiencing a major shift in your consciousness. The Hanged Man asks you to be open to the unknown, and to accept the changes that are happening in your life. The Hanged Man assures you that these changes are for your highest good, and that they will lead you to a deeper understanding of yourself and your purpose.

The Hanged Man is not a card of doom or despair, but rather a card of hope and liberation. It encourages you to look at your situation from a different angle, and to find the hidden opportunities and blessings that are waiting for you. The Hanged Man reminds you that sometimes you have to lose something in order to gain something better.

The Meaning of Death Arcana Tarot Card in Readings

The meaning of the Death card in the Major Arcana, which is one of the most misunderstood and feared cards in the deck.

The Death card does not necessarily mean physical death, although it can sometimes indicate a major transformation or ending in your life. The Death card represents change, renewal, rebirth, and letting go of the old to make way for the new. It can also signify a transition from one phase or stage of life to another, such as a career change, a relocation, a divorce, or a spiritual awakening.

The Death card invites you to embrace the inevitable changes that are happening or will happen in your life, and to see them as opportunities for growth and evolution. It also encourages you to release any attachments, habits, beliefs, or patterns that are no longer serving you or holding you back. By doing so, you will create space for new possibilities and experiences that align with your true self and purpose.

The Death card is not a negative or scary card, but rather a symbol of transformation and renewal. It can be a powerful and positive message if you are willing to face your fears and accept the changes that are coming your way.

The Meaning of Temperance Arcana Tarot Card in Readings

The Temperance card represents balance, harmony, moderation, and patience. It shows a winged angel pouring water from one cup to another, symbolizing the blending of opposites and the alchemical process of transformation. The angel has one foot on land and one in water, indicating the integration of the material and spiritual realms. The card also has a triangle inside a square on the angel's chest, representing the union of fire and water, and a path leading to the mountains in the background, suggesting a journey of personal growth.

When the Temperance card appears in a reading, it suggests that you are finding a middle way between extremes and achieving a sense of equilibrium. You are learning to compromise, cooperate, and harmonize with others, as well as yourself. You are also developing self-control, discipline, and moderation in all aspects of your life. You are avoiding excesses and indulgences, and instead opting for a more balanced and healthy lifestyle.

The Temperance card also indicates that you are undergoing a process of healing and transformation. You are integrating different parts of yourself and becoming more whole and complete. You are also tapping into your inner wisdom and intuition, and finding creative solutions to your problems. You are experiencing a flow of energy and harmony in your life, and feeling more aligned with your true purpose.

The Temperance card is a positive and uplifting card that encourages you to seek balance, harmony, moderation, and patience in your life. It also invites you to embrace change and transformation, and to trust your inner guidance.

The Meaning of The Devil Arcana Tarot Card in Readings

The Devil is one of the most misunderstood cards in the tarot deck. It does not mean that you are doomed or that you have to succumb to evil temptations. Rather, it represents the shadow side of yourself, the aspects that you may deny, repress, or fear. The Devil card challenges you to confront these aspects and integrate them into your whole self.

The Devil card can also indicate a situation where you feel trapped, restricted, or powerless. You may feel like you have no choice or control over your circumstances. This can be a result of external factors, such as a toxic relationship, a stressful job, or a bad habit. Or it can be a result of your own mindset, such as limiting beliefs, low self-esteem, or negative thoughts.

The Devil card invites you to examine what is holding you back and how you can free yourself from it. It asks you to take responsibility for your actions and choices, and to acknowledge the consequences of them. It also encourages you to seek help from others if you need it, and to avoid isolating yourself or becoming dependent on something or someone.

The Devil card is not a sign of doom, but a sign of empowerment. It shows you that you have the power to overcome your challenges and transform your life for the better. It reminds you that you are not a victim, but a creator of your own destiny.

The Meaning of The Tower Arcana Tarot Card in Readings

The Tower is one of the most dramatic and powerful cards in the tarot deck. It represents sudden change, upheaval, crisis, revelation, and liberation. The Tower shows a tall structure being struck by lightning, causing it to crumble and fall. People are seen falling from the tower, symbolizing the loss of security, stability, and comfort.

The Tower card can have both positive and negative meanings, depending on the context and the outcome of the situation. On one hand, The Tower can indicate a shocking event that disrupts your life and forces you to face the truth. This can be a painful and traumatic experience, but it can also lead to a breakthrough and a new perspective. The Tower can also signify that you are breaking free from old patterns, beliefs, or structures that no longer serve you. You may be undergoing a radical transformation that opens up new possibilities and opportunities.

When The Tower appears in a reading, it advises you to be prepared for change and to embrace it as an opportunity for growth. The Tower can also warn you to avoid being rigid, arrogant, or complacent, as these attitudes can make you more vulnerable to the impact of The Tower. The Tower challenges you to face your fears and to trust that the universe has a higher plan for you.

The Meaning of The Star Arcana Tarot Card in Readings

The Star is one of the most positive and hopeful cards in the tarot deck. It represents a time of healing, renewal, and inspiration. The Star shows that you have a connection to the divine and that you are guided by your intuition and higher purpose. The Star also indicates that you have a vision for your future and that you are ready to manifest your dreams.

When the Star appears in a reading, it is a sign of optimism, faith, and confidence. The Star encourages you to trust in yourself and the universe, and to follow your inner light. The Star also suggests that you are receiving blessings and opportunities from the cosmos, and that you should be open to receive them. The Star is a card of hope, joy, and fulfillment.

The Star can also indicate that you are going through a period of healing and recovery after a difficult or traumatic experience. The Star shows that you have overcome the challenges and that you are ready to move forward with a positive outlook. The Star can also signify that you are cleansing yourself of negative energies and emotions, and that you are restoring your balance and harmony.

The Star is a card of spiritual guidance and enlightenment. The Star invites you to explore your spirituality and to connect with your higher self. The Star can also represent a spiritual mentor or teacher who can help you on your journey. The Star can also suggest that you are developing your psychic abilities or receiving messages from the spirit realm.

The Star is a card of creativity and expression. The Star shows that you have a unique talent or gift that you can share with the world. The Star encourages you to express yourself freely and authentically, and to let your light shine. The Star can also indicate that you are involved in a creative project or activity that brings you joy and satisfaction.

The Star is a card of love and compassion. The Star shows that you have a loving and generous heart, and that you are willing to help others in need. The Star also suggests that you are attracting love and kindness into your life, and that you are experiencing harmony and peace in your relationships. The Star can also signify a soulmate connection or a spiritual bond with someone special.

The Meaning of The Moon Arcana Tarot Card in Readings

The Moon is one of the most mysterious and powerful cards in the Major Arcana of the Tarot. It represents the subconscious, intuition, dreams, illusions, fears and secrets. The Moon invites you to explore the hidden realms of your psyche and to trust your inner guidance.

When The Moon appears in a reading, it may indicate that you are facing some confusion, deception or uncertainty in your life. You may not have all the information you need, or you may be misled by your own emotions or fantasies. The Moon challenges you to look beyond the surface and to trust your intuition, even if it contradicts what you see or hear.

The Moon can also signify a time of creativity, imagination and psychic development. You may be drawn to artistic, spiritual or mystical pursuits that help you express your inner vision. The Moon encourages you to follow your dreams and to listen to your inner voice.

The Moon is a card of transformation, as it reflects the cycles of nature and life. The Moon reminds you that nothing is permanent and that everything changes. You may be going through a period of transition, growth or healing that requires you to face your fears and embrace your true self.

The Moon is a card of mystery, magic and intuition. It invites you to dive deep into your subconscious and to discover the hidden treasures within. The Moon asks you to trust your instincts and to follow your heart.

The Meaning of The Sun Arcana Tarot Card in Readings

The Sun is the nineteenth card of the Major Arcana and represents joy, success, and enlightenment. It is a card of optimism, vitality, and confidence. The Sun symbolizes the source of life and energy, as well as the inner light that guides us to our true self. The Sun also signifies clarity, honesty, and freedom from illusions.

When the Sun appears in a reading, it indicates a positive outcome, a happy situation, or a favorable circumstance. It suggests that you are experiencing or will experience a period of happiness, fulfillment, and satisfaction in your life. You may have achieved a goal, overcome a challenge, or realized a dream. You may also feel more confident, creative, and expressive. The Sun encourages you to enjoy the present moment and celebrate your achievements.

The Sun can also indicate a new level of awareness, understanding, or insight. You may have gained a clearer perspective on your life purpose, your relationships, or your personal growth. You may have discovered something new about yourself or the world around you. The Sun invites you to embrace your true self and share your light with others. It also reminds you to be grateful for the blessings in your life and to radiate positivity and warmth.

The Meaning of The Judgment Arcana Tarot Card in Readings

The Judgment card is one of the most powerful and mysterious cards in the Major Arcana. It represents a moment of awakening, transformation, and rebirth. It can also signify a call to action, a decision, or a final verdict.

In readings, the Judgment card can indicate that you are ready to face the consequences of your past actions, whether good or bad. You may be feeling a sense of closure, completion, or liberation. You may also be experiencing a spiritual awakening, a new perspective, or a higher purpose.

The Judgment card can also challenge you to make a choice that will affect your future. You may be faced with a moral dilemma, a career change, or a relationship issue. You may need to forgive yourself or others, or to accept responsibility for your mistakes. You may also need to heed a call to follow your true passion, your inner voice, or your divine guidance.

The Judgment card is not about judgment in the negative sense, but rather about discernment, evaluation, and discernment. It asks you to be honest with yourself and others, to align your actions with your values, and to live authentically and ethically. It also invites you to embrace change, growth, and renewal.

The Judgment card is a powerful reminder that you have the power to shape your destiny. It urges you to rise above your fears, doubts, and limitations, and to trust in your potential and purpose. It also assures you that you are not alone in this journey, but that you are guided and supported by a higher force.

The Meaning of The World Arcana Tarot Card in Readings

The World is the final card of the Major Arcana, and it represents the completion of a cycle, the achievement of a goal, or the fulfillment of a destiny. It is a card of wholeness, harmony, and integration. The World also signifies travel, expansion, and exploration. It can indicate that you are ready to move on to a new phase of your life, or that you have reached a level of mastery in your field.

The World can also symbolize the connection between the physical and the spiritual realms, as well as the unity of all living beings. It shows that you have a cosmic perspective, and that you are aware of your place in the universe. You have transcended the limitations of your ego, and you are in tune with your higher self. You have a sense of gratitude, joy, and peace.

The World is a very positive card, and it suggests that you have everything you need to succeed. You have learned the lessons of the previous cards, and you have grown as a person. You have overcome challenges, and you have gained wisdom and experience. You are ready to celebrate your achievements, and to share your gifts with others. You are also open to new opportunities, and to embrace change. The World is a card of completion, but also of new beginnings.

THE FOOL

THE MAGICIAN

THE HIGH PRIESTESS

THE EMPRESS

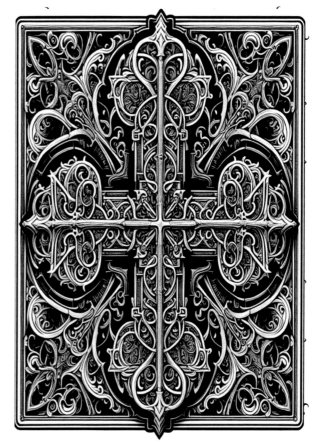

THE EMPEROR

THE HIEROPHANT

THE LOVERS

THE CHARIOT

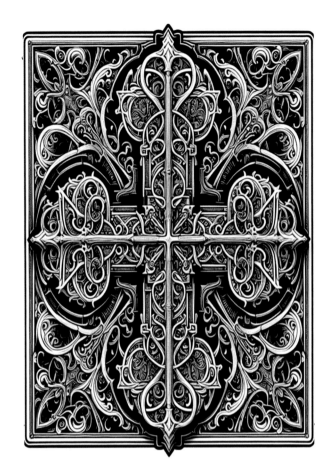

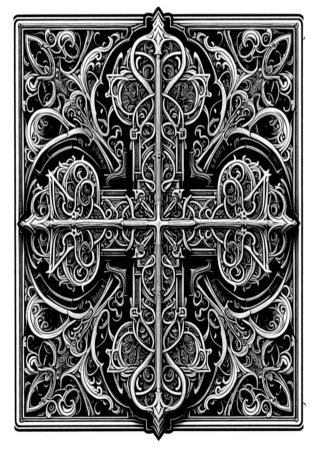

STREANGTH

THE HERMIT

WHEEL OF FORTUNE

JUSTICE

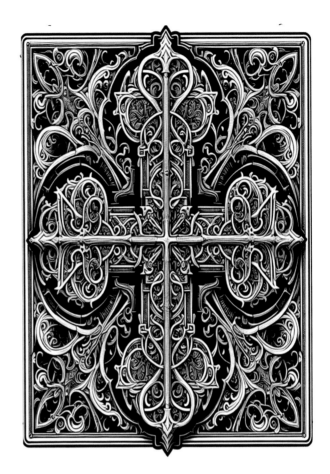
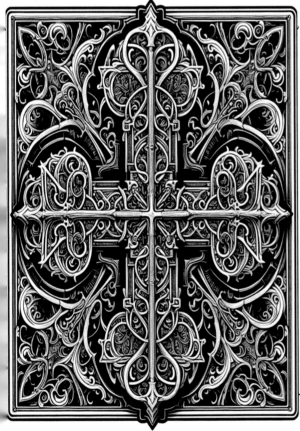

THE HANGED MAN

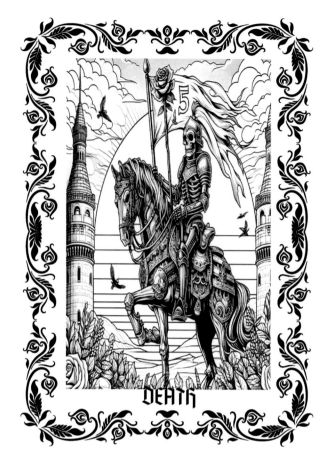

DEATH

TEMPERANCE

THE DEVIL

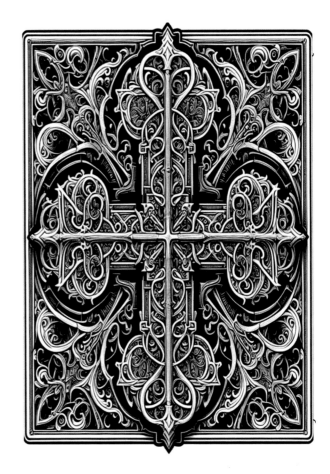
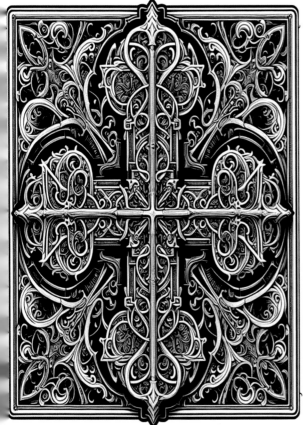

THE TOWER

THE STAR

THE MOON

THE SUN

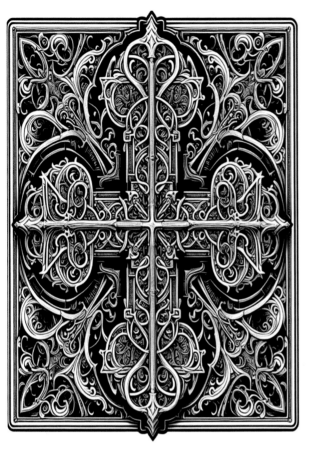
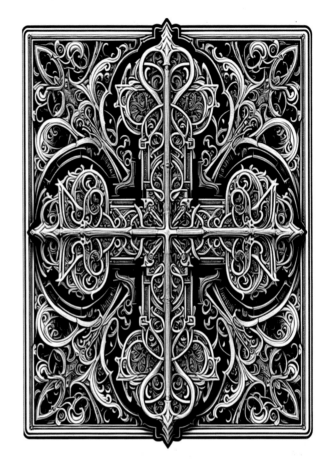
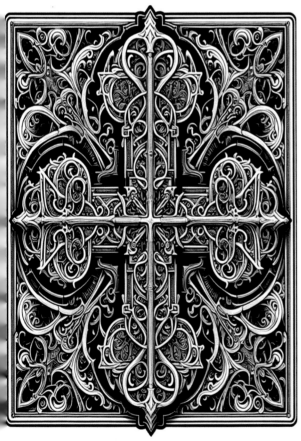

JUDGMENT

WORLD

THE WORLD

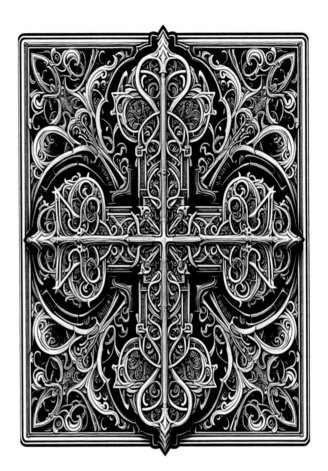

7 STEPS GUIDE ON HOW TO DO A TAROT READING ON YOURSELF

1. Relax Begin your tarot card reading by focusing on relaxation. This initial step is crucial, especially if you're seeking guidance during challenging times or feeling stressed about the future. Temporarily setting aside intense emotions allows you to concentrate on your queries and aids in developing emotional management skills.

2. Choose a Spread
Selecting a spread is the next step in conducting a tarot reading for yourself. Options include a 3-card, 5-card, 10-card, or even a 20-card spread. For beginners, the 3-card spread is recommended as it provides effective answers without overwhelming interpretation challenges.
This versatile spread can be used to inquire about various aspects of your life, such as past, present, future, as well as delving into situations, actions, potential outcomes, you, your partner, your relationship, dreams, challenges, tips on managing them, and weaknesses and strengths with advice on how to balance them.

3. Asking Questions, the Right Way
Many individuals mistakenly believe that tarot cards can predict specific dates or provide yes/no answers. However, this approach is not ideal for tarot card readings, as the cards are meant to weave a narrative and offer insights. Since tarot cards are connected to various aspects of your life, including your life path, relationships, challenges, emotions, and dreams, expecting fixed answers can be limiting.
To respect and connect with tarot cards effectively, it's crucial to ask questions in the right way. Consider the following when formulating questions for a self-tarot reading:
- What do I need to know about today, my job, my partner, my love life, my health, etc.?
- What kind of energetic vibes are emanating from this situation, person, or dream?
- How can I achieve my desires?
- How can I create my dream life?
Personally, I prefer to jot down my questions in a journal before shuffling the tarot cards. This practice helps me stay relaxed and focused during the reading.

4. Shuffle and Lay Down the Cards (Face Down) to Uncover Their Message

After shuffling the cards, posing your questions, and laying them face down, it's time to reveal their message. Explore how the cards connect with each other, assess your feelings toward each card, and consider how the reading resonates with you. Tarot cards not only provide answers but also encourage introspection, prompting you to delve into your life at a deeper level. By embracing the magical power of tarot cards, you can let down your walls, acknowledge your true self, and discover what you genuinely desire.

5. Unveiling the Story Behind the Cards

For additional guidance during your tarot card reading, you can refer to a book, often provided with specific card decks. If you seek further support, stay tuned, as we will soon release card meanings to aid your exploration of tarot cards.

To narrate the story, follow these steps:
- Treat each card as an individual entity.
- Recognize the combinations of cards and their relevance to your question.
- Take note of recurring numbers, themes, or suits.
- Write down your interpretation of what the cards are conveying.

If you find it challenging to grasp the message:

Stay calm and refrain from assuming there's an issue with your reading. When the interpretation seems unclear, take a moment to slow down the process. Remember, there's no right or wrong in tarot readings; an unconventional reading may suggest you're not yet prepared to comprehend the message.

If faced with ambiguity, keep the spread visible throughout the day. Return to it when things seem unclear, allowing time for your mind to clear. Often, the cards' message becomes apparent when you are more receptive.

6. Interpreting the Cards in Your Unique Way

While having a guide is beneficial, don't limit yourself to interpreting tarot readings solely based on books or external sources. The most authentic source for interpreting a self-done tarot reading is unlocking your intuition and letting your mind and spirit guide you in unveiling the cards' messages.

Developing this intuitive connection takes time. Begin somewhere, and as you spend more time with your cards, you'll establish a deeper connection and a unique bond with them.

7. Embrace the Journey
The key to mastering the art of reading tarot cards lies in relishing the experience of conducting readings on yourself. Allow the cards the opportunity to unveil more about your life path, challenges, past, present, and future. Engage in repeated tarot readings, particularly on yourself, to immerse yourself in a magical energetic flow characterized by love, respect, and trust in the power of tarot cards. Keep in mind that while having plans, don't be rigid in expecting them to unfold precisely as envisioned.

Guide on Tarot:
Performing Tarot Readings on Your Own

Can beginners engage in self Tarot spreads? Definitely! Tarot serves as a tool to enhance understanding of our present circumstances, acknowledge intuition, and predict possible outcomes. While it may appear intimidating, the process is straightforward. Let me guide you through it.

Purifying Your Environment's Energy
Before embarking on our reading, set the stage for your space (both physically and mentally). Purify the atmosphere by burning herbs, ringing a bell or chimes, indulging in a bath, or utilizing your preferred crystals.

(I personally favor a Selenite wand, a superb energy revitalizer known for enhancing clarity; it can be easily and effectively waved over the space, the cards, and your body). Once the energy is purified, find a comfortable spot where you can conduct your ritual without disturbance. Close your eyes, clear away mental clutter, and envision a shield of protective energy enveloping you.

Shuffling and choosing the cards

Engage in a few deep breaths, inhaling through your nose and exhaling through your mouth. While practicing this, focus on your question or the guidance you seek, maintaining an open mind and heart to receive insights from the cards. Once prepared, open your eyes and shuffle the deck, concentrating on your inquiry. Remember, there's no incorrect way to shuffle. When you sense the cards are well-mixed (you'll instinctively know!), begin laying them out in front of you. This arrangement is known as a "spread," and the card distribution and positions influence the meaning, forming combinations that contribute to the overall response to your question.

It's advantageous to decide on the spread before shuffling, but be open to drawing additional cards for clarity or starting anew with a different question as needed.

Pro tip: Avoid repeatedly asking the same question, as it can lead to confusion. If dissatisfied with the answer received, resist the temptation to restart and draw new cards until a different outcome appears (which is unlikely). Instead, consider accepting the insights provided, recognizing them as a deeper understanding of your current situation. Remember, nothing is predetermined, and you hold the authority to plan your next steps based on this guided wisdom.

Choosing a spread

Purifying Your Environment's Energy

Before embarking on our reading, set the stage for your space (both physically and mentally). Purify the atmosphere by burning herbs, ringing a bell or chimes, indulging in a bath, or utilizing your preferred crystals.

(I personally favor a Selenite wand, a superb energy revitalizer known for enhancing clarity; it can be easily and effectively waved over the space, the cards, and your body). Once the energy is purified, find a comfortable spot where you can conduct your ritual without disturbance. Close your eyes, clear away mental clutter, and envision a shield of protective energy enveloping you.

When selecting a spread, consider how in-depth you want your answer to be. The more cards drawn, the more intricate the insights. As a general guideline, a three or five-card spread is recommended for clarity without overwhelming complexity. I suggest interpreting each card individually based on its placement, then examining how they collectively weave into a comprehensive narrative with layered meanings.

There's an ongoing debate in the Tarot community regarding reading card reversals (when a card is dealt upside down). Reversals can draw attention to something specific and may indicate the opposite of the card's upright meaning. In some instances, a reversed card may not significantly alter the overall meaning but instead highlight a lack of that energy.

However, it can also introduce a completely different interpretation or none at all. Due to the potential confusion, it's advisable to initially focus on the upright meanings of each card. As you grow more familiar with the language of Tarot, you can explore reversal meanings in your ongoing Tarot journey. With increased experience and intuition, you'll confidently discern when to give importance to a reversal or disregard it.

When formulating your question, consider moving away from "yes/no" inquiries and opt for a more open-ended approach. For instance, rather than asking, "Will I get the promotion at work?" pose a question like, "What obstacles are impeding my career advancement?" Phrasing your question in this manner encourages deeper insight and reflection, providing a more nuanced answer that surpasses the simplicity of a "yes" or "no."

Types of Tarot reads
Past, present, and future

For beginners delving into Tarot spreads, a recommended starting point is a straightforward three or five-card spread. These spreads, commonly themed around gaining clarity in areas such as work, love, or spiritual purpose, offer insights based on the number of cards drawn.

A three-card spread typically explores past, present, and future energies relevant to your current situation. On the other hand, a five-card spread expands on this by not only addressing the temporal aspects but also highlighting potential obstacles and offering supplementary advice to guide you toward a resolution.

3-card relationship spread

One of my preferred relationship spreads involves drawing three cards for a quick and insightful energetic assessment of a situation. This versatile spread can be applied to romantic relationships, friendships, work connections, or any partnership scenario to provide a deeper understanding of the energy surrounding the connection.

I

n this spread, the first card pulled signifies your energy in relation to the other person. The second card reflects the energy of the other person in relation to you. The third and final card represents the combined energy of the partnership. This spread proves valuable when someone appears distant, or when you sense a change in dynamics. It offers information to help you gain insight before engaging in honest and open communication with the other person. After all, progress is often hindered without mutual dialogue, where feelings and perspectives can be shared openly.

12-card general read

For a comprehensive overview of the year ahead, consider using a twelve-card spread, with each card representing the energetic theme of a specific month. This versatile spread can be employed either before the commencement of a calendar year or on your own "personal new year" around your birthday. It serves to unveil lessons to be learned, potential obstacles to be mindful of, and offers guidance for your long-term goals. The cards drawn for each month provide insights into the overarching themes that may shape your journey throughout the year.

The Celtic Cross

When faced with a complex question that demands significant insight, it's time to delve into the classic Celtic Cross spread, comprised of ten cards, to arrive at your final resolution. This widely recognized and extensively used spread offers a comprehensive and intricate examination of the situation. I suggest gradually working your way up to this spread as you become more comfortable with your Tarot skills. The Celtic Cross allows for gathering insights from various angles, making it a versatile framework that can be employed even without a specific query in mind. Sit back, relax, and let the cards reveal their messages to you in the present moment!

In the Celtic Cross spread, the first six cards are arranged in a cross shape, symbolizing the current issue at hand. The remaining four cards form a vertical line, offering insights into additional influences surrounding the main concern. This layout allows for a detailed exploration of the complexities and various aspects associated with the question or situation, providing a comprehensive understanding of the factors at play.

n this spread, the first card pulled signifies your energy in relation to the other person. The second card reflects the energy of the other person in relation to you. The third and final card represents the combined energy of the partnership. This spread proves valuable when someone appears distant, or when you sense a change in dynamics. It offers information to help you gain insight before engaging in honest and open communication with the other person. After all, progress is often hindered without mutual dialogue, where feelings and perspectives can be shared openly.

12-card general read

For a comprehensive overview of the year ahead, consider using a twelve-card spread, with each card representing the energetic theme of a specific month. This versatile spread can be employed either before the commencement of a calendar year or on your own "personal new year" around your birthday. It serves to unveil lessons to be learned, potential obstacles to be mindful of, and offers guidance for your long-term goals. The cards drawn for each month provide insights into the overarching themes that may shape your journey throughout the year.

The Celtic Cross

When faced with a complex question that demands significant insight, it's time to delve into the classic Celtic Cross spread, comprised of ten cards, to arrive at your final resolution. This widely recognized and extensively used spread offers a comprehensive and intricate examination of the situation. I suggest gradually working your way up to this spread as you become more comfortable with your Tarot skills. The Celtic Cross allows for gathering insights from various angles, making it a versatile framework that can be employed even without a specific query in mind. Sit back, relax, and let the cards reveal their messages to you in the present moment!

In the Celtic Cross spread, the first six cards are arranged in a cross shape, symbolizing the current issue at hand. The remaining four cards form a vertical line, offering insights into additional influences surrounding the main concern. This layout allows for a detailed exploration of the complexities and various aspects associated with the question or situation, providing a comprehensive understanding of the factors at play.

1. **Present** - Represents the current situation and the current state of mind of the querent.
2. **Past** - Illuminates past events that have influenced and led to the present situation.
3. **Challenge** - Identifies the current challenge that must be addressed and resolved to move forward.
4. **Future** - Indicates the most likely short-term outcome if the current situation remains unchanged.
5. **Conscious** - Points to the querent's goals, desires, and assumptions regarding the present situation.
6. **Unconscious** - Reveals the feelings, beliefs, and values driving the current situation, often uncovering hidden surprises of significant value.
7. **Your Influence** - This card reveals how your perception of the situation influences the potential outcome. It can also provide advice on how to proceed based on your understanding.
8. **External Influence** - Highlights how the world around you and the perceptions of others can impact your situation, factors beyond your immediate control.
9. **Hopes and Fears** - Offers insights into how the querent's outlook is influencing the outcome. It's important to note that hopes and fears are often intertwined, providing a nuanced understanding.
10. **Outcome** - If the current course of action is maintained, this card represents the most likely resolution to the situation, offering a glimpse into the potential final outcome.

As you continue practicing, reading the cards will become easier and more intuitive. However, there are situations, especially those with personal attachments or complexity, where everyone may feel stuck. In such cases, it's advisable to seek the assistance of a professional who can provide perspective without personal bias. While the cards offer valuable insight and guidance, it's crucial to remember that your actions based on this information ultimately shape your destiny. The cards serve as a tool, and how you interpret and apply their guidance plays a pivotal role in determining your outcomes.

I would like to convey my heartfelt gratitude to all my readers who have chosen to invest in my Tarot Card coloring book, Chroma Tarot. Your decision to purchase this book means a great deal to me, and I sincerely hope that your experience with it is nothing short of wonderful. In a world filled with countless options, I am genuinely thankful that you have opted for this particular creation. Chroma Tarot is not just a coloring book; it serves as a comprehensive guide to understanding the art of tarot reading and delving into the intricate meanings behind each tarot card. Once again, thank you for your support and trust in my work. At the bottom of this page, you'll find a barcode. I invite you to scan it with your device. If you've enjoyed the journey through Chroma Tarot, I'd like to kindly ask for a small favor in return. Would you consider taking just a couple of minutes to leave a review for this book on Amazon? Your feedback is incredibly valuable to me, as it not only aids in refining this book but also guides me in crafting future works on topics that may pique your interest. Thank you sincerely for your support and for being a part of this creative journey with me.
J.C Mendryga

SCAN ME

Made in the USA
Las Vegas, NV
23 February 2024

86183744R00062